T0120700

THE SEARCH
FOR THE
BIBLICAL MARRIAGE CEREMONY

WHILE CLEAVING TO THE SEEDS OF GENESIS

B ELANE

WESTBOW
PRESS®
A DIVISION OF THOMAS NELSON
& ZONDERVAN

WestBow Press books may be ordered through booksellers or by contacting:

WestBow Press
A Division of Thomas Nelson & Zondervan
1663 Liberty Drive
Bloomington, IN 47403
www.westbowpress.com
844-714-3454

ISBN: 978-1-6642-8978-9 (sc)
ISBN: 978-1-6642-8977-2 (e)

Print information available on the last page.

WestBow Press rev. date: 02/20/2023

CONTENTS

INTRODUCTION

In today's world, anything goes. Everyone is entitled to believe whatever they wish. When it comes to marriage, the other partner can be a dog, cat, or dolphin. And homosexuals can even marry other homosexuals. We have forgotten what marriage is and what it represents. God made marriages for His people. Period. The ones that know Him and want to follow His laws to the best of their ability.

People who are not Christians, or people who do not know God, do not want to follow His laws of nature that HE put in place for all mankind at the beginning of time. They follow their directions and pollute the rules that have been in place since Genesis 1. They do things that the people of old did when they worshiped false gods. They were having sex with multiple partners at one time, getting pregnant, having babies, and throwing their newborns into the burning fire for a sacrifice to their false fertility god Moloch or some other god. They believed their gods would give them abundant crops if they gave their infant child as a sacrifice to his burning fires.

Today the same thing is happening. Marrying and remarrying; having abortions to eliminate any inconvenience of self-indulgence. The Bible foretells all of this (2 Timothy. 3:1-5), and as a Christian nation today, we should not have forgotten what marriage is or what it is all about.

When I first moved out of my family's protection, I met a woman living with her boyfriend. I asked her when she and her boyfriend were planning on getting married. She promptly told me that marriage was something man thought up. It was not biblical. The Lord usually gave me answers to questions or statements like this. But for some reason, God was strangely quiet. I, therefore, started searching and digging into the Bible for a Biblical wedding ceremony. But for some reason, the Lord did not help me with this acquisition, and for years, I have searched, trying to find that answer. All I could find was the marriage supper, the wedding night, and the wedding party. There was nothing on a biblical wedding ceremony—or so I thought at the time.

I am a person who believes the Bible holds the key to every answer, and I cannot let it go until the Lord revealed the answer to me. If a person genuinely seeks an answer to something, you had better put your seat belt on, for you will not know where the Lord might lead you. If you are pretty set on your beliefs like I was, it might take DECADES before He can break through a thick skull.

QUESTIONNAIRE

To make things interesting before you read this book, take this quick questionnaire. Write the answer in your own words. There is no wrong answer. Put your answers in a sealed envelope. You could even use your envelope as your bookmarker. Once you have finished reading this book, open your envelope and see if any of your viewpoints might have changed. You may be surprised. You may have a deeper understanding of why you believe the way you do.

1. In Genesis 2:18, 20, what does a helpmete or helpmate mean?
2. In Genesis 2:24, what does it mean to you when you read, "A man should cleave unto his wife, and they shall be one flesh?"
3. What is the Marriage Ceremony in the Old Testament?
4. What is the purpose of marriage?
5. How old should one be to marry, in your eyes?
6. How do you feel about homosexuality? And why?
7. How do you feel about a much older person marrying a much younger person (Male or female)?
8. What does a covenant mean, and its purpose?
9. How do you feel about couples living together without a marriage license?
10. What is the purpose of asking the father for the daughter's hand in marriage?

PROLOGUE

THE SECRET
(The characters in this story are entirely fictional. Any resemblance to actual persons living or dead, is entirely coincidental)

The old lady sat at the kitchen table in her home, looking out the window. She was in her golden years and could see that her time on earth was short. She was pushing 80, and she had been holding onto a deep, dark secret that her children did not know.

It was much easier to keep the secret when their dad was alive. At least she had someone to share it with, but he had died over 25 years ago, leaving her with this heavy burden. As the years went by, it had gotten harder to hold on to without anyone to share it with. Should she tell her children while she still could? Once she was gone, the secret surely would come out, and who would be able to tell her side of the story?

Her mind wandered to her early school days when she met her best friend, Jimmy. They were playmates in grade school and inseparable throughout their Junior and Senior High School years. If you saw one, you saw the other. It was no surprise to anyone when Jim asked her father for her hand in marriage. Of course, her father said yes, since he practically lived in their home and was already considered family--and she was with his family.

The wedding was on, and there was a flurry of preparations and activities after her father said yes. She and her family were taking care of the wedding preparation, and Jim was fixing and moving their things to their new apartment.

Being so stressed out on the eve of the wedding, we decided to disappear for a couple of hours to decompress at our favorite spot before becoming husband and wife. Being together for so long, we were comfortable in each other's company. Words were not needed to know what the other was thinking or feeling. We just enjoyed being together. I remember laying my head on his shoulder, feeling contentment, and feeling him relax, as he laid his head on hers.

The next thing we saw was the sun trying to come up over the horizon. We had fallen asleep! Jim tried to get me to my parent's house before anyone noticed I was missing. But every light in the house was on when we got there. Sneaking in quietly was impossible, so the direct approach was decided. After all, it was our wedding day.

As soon as we entered the house, the men started shaking Jim's hand and patting him on the back, shoving money into his hand. The women all started hugging and crying simultaneously, and then we were being pushed out the door toward Jim's car. If we had just said something then, she wouldn't be carrying this heavy secret, for everyone assumed they had eloped! No one had even asked to see the marriage license. But Jim and I were so young then and too embarrassed to speak up. Once thing settled down with their friends and family, they would go before the "Justice of the Peace" and get married. But things didn't seem to work out that way.

Jim started a new job that placed demands on him, and then the babies started coming, which meant Jim had to take on an extra job to make ends meet.

One important thing that Jim and I were adamant about was raising our children in a church. We found one we both enjoyed and later joined. Eventually, the church members ask Jim to be one of their Deacons, and even though we both felt like frauds, he accepted. Our little family kept growing while attending that church. Our oldest son became a pastor of his own church, one of our daughters married a young man from the church, that later became one of their

Deacon, and our other daughter became the church's music director. Our youngest son was at the age of needing a man in his life when his dad died and the church's youth pastor stepped in to take the place of that man. I guess that is why our youngest son decided to became a youth minister.

Their dad was a good, hard-working man who loved his family passionately. She would hate for any of them to think badly of him, and she was honored to have spent most of her life with him, even though they never got married. She hoped he made it to heaven, for if he had not, then she wouldn't be going to heaven either.

The old lady continued sitting at the kitchen table, looking out the window. She still had not come any closer to what she should do about this secret. Should she tell her children that their parents never got married? Or not?

PREFACE

THE SEARCH FOR THE
BIBLICAL WEDDING CEREMONY

I was nineteen when I started community college, away for the first time from the all-seeing eyes of my parents, and after 12 long years of school, I was not interested in studying. I found out later that my dad sent me to college to find a husband. I made new friends on the college campus, and not all of them were Christians. One young woman who was a self-proclaimed atheist and living with her boyfriend piqued my interest when she told me that the marriage ceremony, as we know it, was man-made.

Growing up in a Christian community, where everyone was married once, divorce was uncommon, and 50th anniversaries were quite common. Living together was unheard of until you made wedding vows before God. If there was a divorce, people deemed them ruined. If a woman became pregnant before marriage, she became an outcast in the community unless the child's father married her. And I was related to most of the people in that community. Therefore, that one comment by one young woman started a 35-year-plus search for the Biblical Wedding Ceremony.

Before the end of college, I started preparing for my wedding with all the trimmings; a long, beautiful white dress with a long, beautiful veil, bridesmaids, flowers, and the works. It was the most exciting day of my life when my dad walked me down the church aisle toward the man I trusted and loved wholeheartedly. I was ready to start a family with this man, celebrate our 50th anniversary, and share all our special moments without any more separations. I was going to finish my last year of college with him and then start our own life without leaving the other behind. I had not found the Biblical Wedding Ceremony before I walked down the aisle on my dad's arm, but at that moment in time, I did not care. This was how Christian people in a Christian community, in a Christian Nation, got married before God . . . Right?

However, early in our new marriage, I realized I had made a mistake, and I wanted out big time. But we had made a covenant with each other, which meant we also made a covenant with God and I really, Really, REALLY, wanted out. I had no problem breaking my covenant with man, but breaking my covenant with my God caused me to start looking for the Biblical Wedding Ceremony again. And once again, all I could find was the wedding celebration, the wedding supper, and the wedding night. I could not understand why I could not find the wedding ceremony. My mother said you could find everything in the Bible, so why couldn't I find it?

As the years went by, I would pick up the search for the Biblical Wedding Ceremony, especially during challenging times in my life. Still, all I could find was the wedding supper, the wedding celebration, and the wedding night. The Lord kept teaching me, but there was nothing, it seemed, on the Biblical Wedding Ceremony. What was I missing?

Then one day, a young man came knocking on our door asking for our daughter's hand in marriage. I had only seen and heard of this happening one other time when another young man asked my dad for my hand in marriage. I thought it was so romantic and poetic back then, and I still do. After he left I asked my husband why he came to us first before asking our daughter to marry him since she was over eighteen. My husband shrugged and said it was a show of respect toward our daughter and us. I still did not understand but did not say any more.

As our daughter's wedding day drew closer, I found myself thinking of all the events that had led up to this day and all the events with which she was involved. The funny little things she did and said; all her friends she had brought to the house to give them a popsicle; her constant chatter; watching her take the dog for a walk with her roller skates on, but in reality, it was the dog taking her for a roller skate ride through the neighborhood. How did she grow up so fast?

The last few months had been a whirlwind with all the plans she was making, the shopping for the perfect dress, shoes, veil, and things for the wedding and reception; I pondered what she must be feeling right now, both excitement and love for her future husband. I was going to miss all the excitement she had brought to our home; her talent contests, puppet shows for the neighborhood kids, school and church activities, and how could I forget her crying over a misplaced fish she had brought home from a day trip at school? We filled the kid's red wagon up with water for the fish until we could figure out what to do with it. Of course, all the neighborhood boys had to come and look at the fish and pet it. We had to leave the fish in the wagon for an hour to pick up her dad. She couldn't wait to get back home to show him her fish she had caught in the lake. But when we got home, the fish was nowhere in sight. I prayed all night for my daughter's broken heart and for us to find that silly fish in good health. We found it the next day. One of the neighborhood boys saw a cat looking at the fish and was afraid the cat would decide to have it dinner with it, so he took it upon himself to put the fish in his horse trough swimming pool in his back year. She was just a little girl yesterday. And now she is a bride.

Without warning, *"I am a bride, too."* I was shocked! This quiet time was a mother's time to meditate on her daughter leaving the home she had always known. The empty places she was leaving behind—the excitement of her beginning a new adventure, a new chapter, a new life as a new bride with her husband, making their own rules. I did not want to take anything away from my daughter's special day, but I also recognized the Lord's voice when he tried to reveal something. *"Yes, Lord. I am Your Bride,"* I said reverently.

After pondering this for a few seconds, I ask, *"How did I become Your Bride, Lord?"*

I could feel His fatherly love when he asked me, "How is your daughter becoming a bride?" Thinking of the steps she would be taking on her wedding day, I finally answered, *"She will be walking down the aisle on her father's arm,"* I replied, *"before all her friends and family, towards the man she totally loves and trusts, and-OF COURSE,"* I cried excitedly. *"To become your bride, I also had to walk down an aisle before all my friends and spiritual family and profess, verbally to You, who You are and what You mean to me. My daughter must profess the same to her new husband verbally before her family and friends".*

I was so excited. I knew I did not understand everything except the walking down the aisle part. But that was Okay, for God was finally opening the door to the Biblical Wedding Ceremony. Little did I know, He opened the door with a small crack. I still had to get rid of man-made biblical doctrine. Once He started opening the Biblical Marriage Ceremony door, I began understanding why God called certain things abominable in His sight and why man should go and ask the parents for their daughters in marriage.

My parents and grandparents fell asleep, and today their children and grandchildren are just as inquisitive as I was. Still, no one could answer their questions, so parents made up answers that sounded good, letting darkness engulf their children and mankind.

Some people will accept some of what I have learned, but I doubt you will accept it all, which is Okay. Just take what you can digest. My mother cannot digest any of it because she cannot and will not change. She has been indoctrinated all her life, and now she is close to the end. My husband understands and accepts half of what the Lord has shown me but will not go against what man put in place close to one thousand years ago. I hope this journey will be as exciting for you as it has been for me.

I have used several Bible versions to help show a more precise and concise understanding of my journey. Only the bold print items are from specific Bibles listed due to the direct quote associated.

CHAPTER 1

THE WOMAN AT THE WELL

One Sunday morning, I was trying to listen to our Pastor's sermon, but my mind kept wandering away, thinking about who knows what. I was determined to get my mind back on his sermon when he mentioned the woman at the well. Suddenly, I was in the presence of the Lord, for I do not remember anything else from the Pastor's sermon. The Lord started revealing thing I could not believe I had not seen before! Thing I knew but had not connected with the Biblical Wedding Ceremony.

In old Biblical times, a father with a son would go looking for a wife for that son. Once the father found that maiden, the two fathers would negotiate a hefty price for the young girl to wife (Genesis 29: 28 very old King James Version with no date) the son, creating a marriage covenant between the two families. The young girl would stay at her father's house until her new husband built a place to start their new life together and raise their family. But the son's father had "the" say as to when the house was ready for his son to bring his new bride to her new home. When they arrived at their new home, they would immediately start fulfilling their marriage covenant. Instead of a marriage certificate for the young couple to show proof of their marriage, they had their bloody sheets as proof of the purity of their marriage covenant. The girl's parents kept the sheets to protect their daughter and themselves if anyone tried to say anything against their daughter's virtue (Deuteronomy 22: 14-20).

Once the Lord revealed this, the Bible started opening up rapidly. The Lord took me through the Old Testament, then to the New Testament, and then back to the Old Testament again. He took me through it so fast I'm not sure I can reveal it as He did.

Just as God the Father gave Eve's hand to Adam, NOT to be his wife, but TO wife (Genesis 2: 21-25).

Abram's father, Terah, gave his daughter, Sarai, Abram's half-sister, "to wife."(Genesis 20: 12). And Terah gave his granddaughter to his son, Nahor, "to wife," which would be Nahor's niece (I guess Abram's father was unwilling to pay money for a wife for his sons (Genesis 11: 29).

Abraham sent his servant, Eliezer of Damascus (Genesis 15:2), to find a wife for his son, Isaac. He sent camels, jewelry, money, and gold with his servant to negotiate a price for a virtuous young girl (Genesis 24)

Another story the Lord reminded me of was Tamar. Her first two husbands died, and her father-in-law fathered her child (I am not sure where the biblical wedding ceremony was in that story yet (Genesis 38: 6-25).

Jacob gave up fourteen years of his life to pay for his two wives (Genesis 16: 25-30).

However, I am sure the father of the "woman at the well" also made a covenant for his daughter. That would mean her father could not enter another covenant with another family. Therefore, which husband do you think Christ meant for the "woman at the well" to return to?

All this and more came while the Pastor used the "Woman at the Well" in his sermon. I have no idea what the Pastor's sermon was about, but I do know God was in the house, teaching me.

The following Sunday, as my husband and I entered the church, I started visiting with my church sisters in the hallway. As soon as my feet touched the sanctuary floor, the Lord started flashing Biblical couples from last Sunday and more before my eyes again.

Rebecca said "yes" to marrying a stranger she had never met and traveled across the desert with another stranger for a husband (Genesis 24: 57-58).

Also, how could Abraham and Sara's grandson, Jacob, not know that he married Leah first instead of Rachel (Genesis 29: 16-25)?

What about Joseph? How could he have divorced Mary privately if she still lived with her parents? Wouldn't she still be under her parent's protection and not his (Matthew 1:18-25)?

The Bible never mentions any ceremony with Adam and Eve. It just says that God just brought Eve to Adam, but I can imagine that God placed Eve's hand into Adam's hand (Genesis 2:22).

There were others the Lord flashed before my eyes while I tried to converse with my sisters before church started. I finally cried out, "Lord, You showed me last Sunday how two families entered a covenant with their children, but what about the Biblical Marriage Ceremony? I still do not understand!" I could feel the Lord smiling at me as a father would smile at a beloved child and said, "Why don't you start at the beginning?"

OF COURSE! Why hadn't I thought of that?

CHAPTER 2

THE SEEDS OF GENESIS

LET ME TELL YOU
ABOUT THE BIRDS AND THE BEES
THE FLOWERS AND THE TREES
THE MOON UP ABOVE
AND THE THING THEY CALLED
LOVE
("The Birds and the Bees," Herb Newman, 1965)

For most of my life, I have tried to avoid Genesis 1, and I am sure I am not alone. It is so dull and impossible to visualize and understand. For example, in Genesis. 1:6 in the New International Bible, God said, **"Let there be a vault between the waters to separate water from water."** Then the same verse in the English Standard Version, the Bible says, **"Let there be an expanse in the midst of the waters, and let it separate the waters from the waters."** When I got hold of a Christian Standard Bible, I finally understood it was about water and air. Therefore, when God told me to go to the beginning, I thought He was talking about the first married couple. Adam and Eve. Not Genesis One! But when you allow God to work through you, He can open your understanding and show you things you had never seen before. He will make it fun, exciting and straightforward; never dull or confusing. When I finished reading Genesis 1, that silly little song about the birds and the bees kept resounding in my mind about God's creation.

So, let us begin with Genesis 1:2 (The Holy Bible, King James Version) "**. . . the Spirit of God moved upon the face of the waters.**" Everything God touches or makes, there is life. The Bible said that when God's son's blood fell on the ground during His crucifixion, it was so full of energy and life that "**the graves were opened, and many bodies of the saints which slept arose, and come out of the graves . . .**" (Christian Standard Version, Matthews 27:52-53).

When the Spirit touched the face of the waters, I could envision thunder and lightning, like electricity moving in and across the waters, preparing it to hold and sustain life.

There needed to be boundaries for the waters that were full of life, so the Lord formed the earth for those limitations. The ground required the waters to produce its life, but it also needed something else to pull up that life from the ground, so God said, "**let there be light**" and there was light (Genesis 1:3 New Century Version) As an artist prepares his canvas to create a painting, God also had to prepare the waters and the earth for His creation.

God created all kinds of colorful flowers, trees, grass, shrubs, grain, and herbs, on the third day of this brand-new world. Everything He created, He made sure they could create their own seeds to procreate with their kind (Genesis 1: 11-12).

The Lord was light, and everything he created needed light to grow. Therefore, He created two light-bearers to pull up the seeds of the earth: The sun for the day and the moon and stars for the night on the fourth day. I do not know if people realize it, but these magnificent lights still determine our lifestyles to this day through our seasons (Genesis 1: 14-18)

Even though the Lord created the waters and air before the earth, they remained empty of life. On the fifth day (Genesis 1:

20-25), the Lord made diverse types of birds and bees and all sorts of other winged creatures to fill the sky and all kinds of living creatures to fill the seas. Every living creature, whether soaring through the air or gliding through the waters, was created by God, and He made sure all His creatures He created had their very own seeds to procreate with their kind. Now, this is where it gets exciting for me. God blessed all the water animals and told them to fill the seas, and told all the animals that could fly to use their seeds to procreate and have many babies. Did You Get That? He told the animals to use their seeds and create THEIR kind. HE TOLD THEM! The more I thought about the animals that were created on the 5th day, it seemed, most but not all, laid their eggs with their seeds in them.

On the sixth day of creation, I got another surprise. Most everyone knows that God created man from the dust of the earth on that day, but did you know that God created more animals? And He made them, also, from the dust of the earth like Man. God said, "**Let the Earth bring forth living creatures according to their kinds— livestock and creeping things and beasts of the earth according to their kinds.**" (English Standard Version, Genesis 1:24). It was crucial to God that every animal He created could produce its seeds to procreate their kind. Most of these animals, and once again, not all, carried their eggs with seeds in them, until it was time to bring them forth into the world, like man.

The last thing God created on the sixth day, in Genesis 1:25-26 (English Standard Version), was Man. God said, "**Let US make man in OUR image, after Our likeness . . .male and female, he created them.**" If you do not know much about Genesis 1, God created **man**, "male and female." But in Genesis 2, God did not form the female until after he completed the land animals. When God realized that "man," given the tool to be a seed planter, His perfect creation, whom he called Adam, the only creature of his kind, would be alone for the rest of his life if he didn't have a place to plant his seed. And a seed planter that had no one to procreate with was not good and needed to be corrected.

Therefore, God brought all the animals made from the earth's dust and the fowl from the air for man to name, including that crafty serpent. Can you imagine how many animals the man must have seen--and named on the day of his creation?! Yet, none of the animals were worthy of Man to mate with. Without a mate to plant his seed, Adam might try to procreate with the animals, which defiantly would be an abomination to God. Therefore, God had to do something to keep that from happening.

Since none of the animals were good enough for God's perfect creation, He cut open the man and took a rib to create another man (Genesis 2: 21-23). Can you envision the first man waking up and seeing this new creation? The second man? I can almost hear him thinking: "Finally someone like me." But God made this man with a womb that he could produce with, one that could hold his seed and bring it forth into the world. Adam's first words when he saw this new creature were, **"Bone of my bone, flesh of my flesh; she shall be called Woman, for she was taken out from man."** (King James Version, Genesis 1:23)

I do not pretend to understand Adam's words; after all, this is Genesis. I do know what he said must have had a lot of significance to them (it could be good study material). I have my ideas about what it might mean, but I do not want to go to such extremes, for this is not why I am writing this book. Whatever Adam meant when he said those words when he saw Eve, the first woman, she was the perfect help mate. She was "his" helpmate.

God blessed them and said, **"Be fruitful, multiply, fill the earth and subdue it . . ."** (Genesis 1:22 New King James Version). His first command, or law, was the same command he gave to all his creation.

Finally! God had finished the sixth day. I have no idea how long a day is to God. Some say it is a 24-hour period; others say a day to God is one thousand years (2 Peter 3:8). However long it may have been, a lot happened on that sixth day. No wonder God rested on the seventh day. After all that work on the sixth day, I would too!

I finally understood why homosexuality is an abomination to God. The male plants his seeds, he is a seed planter, and the woman is not. No matter how she might try, she cannot plant any of her seeds. Only man.

Once I realized this, I found a male homosexual and asked, "Do you know why men are so special? They are the ones that can plant the seeds of man so the race of man can continue." He gave me such a blank look, and then a light bulb went on over his head.

Then I found a successful working mother with a grown daughter and stated that men were the only ones that could plant their seeds. No matter how she would like to, she cannot plant any of her seeds. She also gave me a blank look, and then a light bulb went on over her head and became unglued. She thought I was saying that man was better than her. That was not what I was saying. I was making a statement. Nothing more and nothing less. After I finally got that across to her, the successful businesswoman sat there with a stunned, surprised look.

It is funny that the sun, moon, and stars still pull the growth from the ground. The grass is still growing, man is still mowing it down, the trees are still producing their fruit, and its grain continues to provide us with loaves of bread and other foods. The animals are still producing to the point that man is trying to keep them from overpopulating their fields. Water is still sustaining everything on the earth, and everything that God created to produce life has stayed the same, except Man, who is trying to change God's laws of nature and commands that He set up from the beginning.

I believe the reason is the lack of understanding of the tool and the womb. That lack of knowledge is why so many single and divorced people have sex outside of marriage, which has nothing to do with procreation.

Kids at schools ask their peers, "How do you know if you are not a homosexual if you haven't tried it?" If our children understood the concept of the "tool and the womb," they may be able to answer that question easier instead of feeling peer pressure.

Homosexuality is exploding in schools. They do not understand that they will die alone if they do not correct their ways of thinking, just like Adam if he had to live without being able to plant his seeds. Thankfully, God did fix the problem and created Eve. Adam would not have started a bloodline if it weren't for Eve, and the homosexual lineage will cease, too, if they continue down the path they are going.

God is a perfect God. When He says something is not good, it is an abomination if not corrected. God created everything from seed time to harvest time-- Plants, animals, and men.

Two males or two females cannot plant and harvest, and they cannot be married in the eyes of God. They may say they are married and even refer to themselves as their "significant" other. But they have too many tools or wombs, which keeps them from procreation.

Luke 13:6-7 tells the story of a man that came to get fruit from a fig tree. After three years, he tells his gardener to cut the fig tree down. It was not bearing any fruit and was not good for anything.

In Matthew 21:18-19, Jesus came across a fig tree with no fruit. Jesus cursed it, and it withered away and died.

Seed time may not be important to man today, but it is to God. Not planting his seeds is dishonorable to God's first command by ending God's good works when he made you perfect in your mother's womb.

I have known married couples who decided not to have children. Is that wrong? I do not know. That will be between them and their God. Paul chose not to marry and have children but instead dedicated his life to Christ. I DO know Paul's (or Saul's) name ceased in his family tree, just as homosexuals will have no one behind them to take their place in their lineage.

There were women in the Bible that would love to have children, like Sarai, Hannah, Anna, John the Baptist's parents, and even Samson's parents. I believe couples unable to have children have an extraordinary calling, especially today, which I will discuss in the next chapter.

Genesis 1 is about seed time. And we need to understand this as we continue our search for the Biblical Wedding Ceremony.

CHAPTER 3

PROCREATION

As I pondered everything the Lord had shown me, I started thinking about all the women in the Bible who were frantic about having children.

There was Sarai, who was so desperate to have a child, she gave another woman to her husband so she could say she gave her husband a child (Genesis 16:1-3).

Jacob's two wives were extremely jealous of each other and gave their maidservants to their husband so that one could provide more children than the other (Genesis 30:1-12).

Naomi is a Hebrew woman living in a foreign land with her husband and two sons. Her sons married Moabite women, and then tragedy struck. Her husband died, and then her two sons. She decided to return to her homeland and did not want her daughters-in-law to go with her, for she could not produce another child for them to have a husband. She was husbandless, childless, and had no grandchildren to give an inheritance to or continue her husband's and sons' names (Ruth 1:3-13).

Remember Hannah (1 Samuel 1)? She appeared not to be able to have children. Her husband's other wife had children and knew how to provoke Hannah into shame and misery for being barren. At one point, Hannah was so ashamed that she went to the temple's steps to pray desperately for a child. She promised the Lord if He would open up her womb for just one child, she would give that child to Him. She gave birth to Samuel, whom she gave to the Priest Eli to raise in the temple when he was two years old.

Then there was Elizabeth, John the Baptist's mother, who gave birth after her childbearing years. When she discovered she was expecting a child, her first comment was, **"Look what the Lord has done for me! My people was ashamed of me, but now the Lord has taken away my shame"** (New Century Version, Luke 1:25, 2022).

And that strange story of Lot and his two daughters, who became pregnant by their father. That is one story I do not want to even think about. But the last line of Genesis 19:32 (King James Version) gives an insight into what was going on with them. The oldest sister said to the younger sister, **". . . that we may preserve seed of our father"**.

My favorite story is of Judah and Tamar (Genesis 38) and his three Canaanite sons, who grew up wild and rowdy. I can imagine Judah believing they would settle down once he found a calm Hebrew wife for his sons, and he found one named Tamar, whom he bought for his oldest son, Er. God hated wicked Er and killed him before he could take his bride out of her parent's house. Tamar became the wife of Onan, Judah's second son. Onan knew if he planted his seed in Tamar, he would not inherit his father's double blessing (Deuteronomy 21: 15-17) as the eldest son. It would go to Tamar's child instead. When Onan entered Tamar, he spilled his seed on the ground so Tamar would not become pregnant, which made God angry; and He killed Onan there on the spot for his evil act (today, it may have been called a heart attack). Tamar had made a covenant with the family of Judah, and Onan had refused to honor it. Since Judah's third son, Shelah was too young for marriage, Judah told Tamar to go back to her father's house until Shelah was of age to marry.

Years later, when Judah's wife died, Shelah had become a grown man and Tamar had to finally admit to herself that Judah was not going to fulfill his covenant by giving his last son to her and therefore be unable to bear a child. The very thing God had made her for. The only way she would be able to have just one child had to come from the family of Judah. He bought her for this reason, and there was no way out of this covenant or to make another covenant with another family. She would become stigmatized as a woman that could not have children. But hers' would be far worse; she would become known as the "black widow of death." Can you imagine a young woman who had two husbands and had died before they could plant their seed in her? She would not allow Judah to do that to her. No, she would not allow that.

When she heard that her father-in-law was going to shear his sheep, she took off her black widow's clothes, dressed up as a prostitute, put a veil over her face so as not to be recognized, and placed herself on the road Judah would be coming down. When Judah saw her, not knowing who she was, and presumed she was a prostitute, he promised her a sheep from his flock if he could come into her. He gave her his signet ring, bracelets, and the staff in his hand to show his word was credible. When Judah returned to pay the prostitute with the sheep and retrieve his things, she had disappeared, and no one knew anything about any prostitute.

Three months later, Judah heard that Tamar was pregnant and wanted to burn her alive at the stake, as was his privilege since she broke their covenant and then he could be rid of her. Tamar produced proof of her child's father, the ring, the bracelets, and the staff. She had tricked Judah into keeping his covenant by planting his seed in her since he had not given her his last son Shelah. Judah never touched Tamar again, but sex was not a big thing like it is today; procreation was. Thankfully, she was determined to preserve the seed of Judah, for she gave birth to twins, one of them being in the lineage of the Messiah.

One more woman I thought of was Anna, a prophetess (Luke 2:36-38).

She had lived with her husband for seven years from her virginity. Which meant she was probably fourteen, as most young women married. During those seven years, she was unable to bring forth children for her husband. After the death of her husband, she went back to her parents, never leaving the temple, praying, and fasting for the rest of her 84 years, for what man, in that day and age, would want a woman that could not bear them children to continue their lineage? Before she died, God honored her by allowing her to see the baby Jesus.

I did not understand why the Lord was showing me all this. What did any of this have to do with the Biblical Marriage Ceremony? Then it slowly started coming together. Could it be so simple? Surely not! No one would believe it! Would they? Could the Biblical Wedding Ceremony be when a man and a woman came together for the first time, not because of fascination or love but to plant their seeds? So, the two can create one? To claim her virginity would account for the blood sacrifice between the covenant of the two families.

The Lord understood my dilemma, for our church had been studying Ray Vander Laan's studies "THAT THE WORLD MAY KNOW." And it just so happened that his teaching was on that very thing. Most of us would dismiss such teachings as a different culture from another time. But God created a culture for His people, and we are His people today. There is a reason He created that culture. Have you seen how out of order our culture is today?

The parents prepared their children early for marriage in Biblical times. They also taught their children a trade, good work ethics, and to be responsible. By the time a son was between twelve to fourteen, he should know his family trade well enough to start his own business or go into business with his father; and man enough to bring his new bride home.

Today, we consider twelve to be a child. If a parent tries to teach a child a trade like mowing grass for a little extra spending money or teach a child to be responsible, it would be considered child slave labor or abuse. By the time children reach eighteen today, there are many unwanted pregnancies, lack of responsibility and seldom and kind of trade skills. When a woman says yes to a man today, it does not mean he can plant his seed in her. If they do get pregnant, they can always get an abortion. I do not know about you, but I see abortion as giving your child to the God of Moloch and throwing your child into the burning fire as a sacrifice to a Canaanite fertility god.

So, we bypass the culture God created when He created the birds and the bees, the flowers, and the trees, and yet they are all still here doing what God ordained them to do. He had a reason and a purpose, and He set laws for everything He created if we look for them and are open enough to accept it. God created man in the beginning also, yet man tries their best to change those laws in a way that does not even look like the laws God created for them. The Sun is still going around the Earth daily, and the moon is still in the sky. The grass still is growing. Farmers are still planting with seeds that their plants produced last year, and all the animals are still producing their kind, as God commanded. Yet Man has forsaken the first law God set for him from the beginning; to procreate and fill the Earth.

People have replaced that law of procreation with the word love; to have an enjoyable time. The rules of God have not changed, but man has twisted them to the point that they are no longer recognizable. Have you heard someone say that God's word and laws "are not meant" to be understood? I have--many times. A lot of God's people, through ignorance, follow the ways of the pagan god Baal. Pleasure; self-gratification; self-seeking; crowd pleasures. I am sure you can think of some. (2 Timothy 3:1-5)

As I said, people do not know God's laws which He has placed for us to follow, because the ways of the world are easier to follow.

CHAPTER 4

THE THING CALLED LOVE

It is hard for most Christians to understand the blood sacrificial covenant in the Old Testament. I do not pretend to understand it myself. Then, one day the Lord started revealing to me that there are still blood covenants in the world today, and it begins with love.

I am not talking about what we think love is. So, what exactly is love? It is used a lot in our daily vocabulary. I love that vase; I love my English teacher; I love the way he speaks; I love that guy or gal, etc.

Before my husband and I were married, we went to a Newly Wed-Nearly Wed Sunday School class. The Sunday School teacher told us that love was not a feeling but an act of the will. I thought, "Okay . . . I can understand that . . . sort of, at least it sounded good".

The day the Lord started dealing with me on this subject, He said, "Love is a covenant word. You made a covenant with Me the day you were baptized. You made a covenant with your husband when you married him. Christ died because He loved you and shed His covenant blood for you, even before you were born. He loved us before we loved him. Once we understood that love, we gave ourselves to Christ Jesus as a young bride (Kallah) gave herself to

her new bridegroom (Ephesians 5:22-23). That is why their wedding
sheets are bloody. It is THEIR sealed covenant blood sacrifice.

Before I go any further, I need to explain the importance of the
word kallah. It is a Hebrew word that means Bride, Crown, Joy,
and Complete. All the terms used for the Bride of Christ. Women
living with their parents in a covenant or living with their husbands,
were called Kallah. Once the man brought his Kallah home, she
was adopted into the family as one of their own, as if she was their
blood. Even though she was not their blood, her blood would mingle
with theirs, with the children she brought into the family. This same
word is how we became adopted into the kingdom of God when
we become Christ's Bride. People that have adopted children can
understand this bond, for they put their heart and soul into that
child, but people that have not adopted a child can understand this
word better as an in-law. This word is used 34 times in the Bible
and 12 books. Some books are Genesis, Ruth, 1 Samuel, Song of
Solomon, and Hosea. I am sure you can think of the great love
stories written in those books and other books in the Bible.

There are at least four types of love found in the bible, and
maybe more, but I will use four.

Agape love is unconditional or selfless love.

Philia love is a brotherly or friendship love.

Storge love is natural, familial love. A love that parents
show to their children and children to their parents.
Or someone that has been married for a long while.

Eros love is an enthusiastic, passionate, romantic
love or sexual attraction. This love is found with
Shechem the Hivite for Dinah in Gen 34. The story
in the book of Ruth with Boaz, Jacob and Rachel,
and David and Bathsheba.

A father looking for a wife for his son wants her to be from a good family. Have a good reputation and is a virgin before he would consider making a covenant with her family and paying a large sum of money for her to be the mother of his grandchildren. When he finds her and makes a transaction, the bloody sheets of the wedding night are a witness that she is all of that. Therefore, her parents keep the sheets as a witness to that covenant.

One of Jacobs' sons, Judah, bought a young, virtuous Hebrew bride for his son, Er. After God killed two of Judah's sons for their evil acts, Judah sent her back to her parent's home until his last son came of age (Genesis 38).

When the young woman saw that Judah had no plans to give her his last son, she tricked Judah into planting his seed in her instead. Judah could do nothing about it for she was more righteous with the blood covenant between the two families than he was. Their marriage was not made in the kind of love we know it to be today. But it was a covenant between them.

Another blood covenant of today is when a baby is born. A child comes into the world through a blood sacrifice or blood covenant. A mother carries a child for nine months, giving her blood to that child. She gets to know her child's personality during those months. Once a woman starts having children, through her blood sacrifices, her body starts dying, and she would not have it any other way. Christ would not have had it any other way, either, sacrificing his blood for us. A mother is bound to her children through her blood sacrifice, and so is Christ through his blood sacrifice. Perhaps that is why children are to honor their parents in God's 5th Commandment.

As I was going over my notes on love, I came across something that had to be from the Lord--before I go any further, I want you to remember I am writing to the Christians only. The non-Christian beliefs are different. We are children of God and should have a distinct set of laws, a different thought process, and a higher standard of living.

The woman was birthed from a man, Adam; therefore, it is

natural for her to mold into her husband's will and begin their lives in marriage. In my humble opinion, this is that inner desire that God placed in women in Gen 3:16.

When a woman gives birth to a child, the baby comes out bloody. Her husband should embrace his wife with deep tenderness and love, for she gave her blood for him at the beginning of their marriage covenant and then for the seeds or children she brings forth into the world. The very definition for "fe" in female or feline means to bring forth.

A young boy (son) will not mold to his parents as a daughter will. That is why the man is what I have always called self-assertive, and the woman birthed by a man (Adam) is not. They become one flesh in marriage by becoming familiar with each other and creating children.

At the beginning of this chapter, I said that our Sunday School teachers noted that love was an act of the will. After being married for over 30 years to the same person and being so opposites, I decided somewhere in our marriage to be happy. I realized I was always focusing on what I believed to be his faults without looking at my own. Now I look upon his faults as his strengths and my strengths as my weakness. I believe he does the same thing with me. What I used to think was love was really infatuation. One day, I looked at him and realized what love really was, and I had those four loves for him. The agape, the philia, the storage, and the eros love. I realized I did not know what love really was when we married. Only when I accepted my husband for who he was, both his goodness and his faults. We are used to each other and comfortable with each other. I am glad I did not leave our marriage when things got rough. Being without my husband now, I would be lonely and lost, and it all started with the act of the will to be happy and to love him unconditionally. This, for me, is "The thing called Love." And perhaps the men and women in the Bible understood this.

For better or for worse
Through sickness and health
Richer or poorer
I will love thee
Until death
Do we part

CHAPTER 5

CLEAVE

Old English, Dutch, Old German, Old Sexton, Old Norse

verb: split or divide, third person present, make a way through forcefully

Also: stick; to cling

Hebrew verb: split, divide, crack, bring forth, slice, stick, gum, join

I was sitting quietly one day thinking about how different my husband and I were. He is the one that keeps people laughing in a crowd; I am the wallflower. He is quick thinking and quick-witted; I am the blond in the group. He likes sports and doing things inside and outside; I can't even throw a ball straight. Duck if I even try to throw something (seriously). At home, he is very organized, and I am very scattered. He is visionary and artistic, whereas I am not so much. He does everything fast, I do everything at a pace. He wants everything now, I want to make plans first. We are truly opposites in every way. Yet he is the most loyal and Godly Man I know. And as much as I hate to admit it, with his fast pace and quick thinking ways, he is always right—most of the time.

My mom and dad were, I don't know if they were as opposite as my husband and me, but they were both headstrong with dominant personalities.

"It takes two to create one," I heard the Lord say. I sat there very quietly and was stunned. Whenever the Lord speaks, you pay attention, for what he usually reveals is so simple that you wonder why you hadn't seen it before. "And the two shall become one," popped into my mind. I have heard preachers say this in wedding ceremonies. Did I read it in the Bible? If so, where? So off to the wonderful invention of the smartphone I go. In Genesis 2:24, when Adam saw the second Man and called her "woman," Adam said, " **Therefore a man shall leave his father and his mother and cleave to his wife; and they shall become one flesh**" (Old King James with no date). The Torah says uses "clings" in place of cleave.

Jesus said the same thing in Matthew 19:5 and Mark 10:8 when the Pharisees questioned Him on divorce. Ephesians 5:31 compares two becoming one flesh as Christ and the church are one.

As I pondered the simplicity of this, I knew that divorce doesn't separate a man and his wife when children are involved. No matter how a person will try to separate their self from a spouse; they will still have memories with the children that became their oneness. They will always share grandchildren; their birthdays, graduation, weddings, and new births will continue in both bloodlines. Even if one of the parents is absent, you can never forget whom you shared that child with and all the memories that go along with them.

How can two people, so opposite, become one? My husband likes to invest in home projects he has going on, and I want to invest for our kids when we are gone. He believed in firm discipline, whereas I was more lenient. He is quick, fast and intense. I am slow and easy going and like to think about things before taking action.

My parents, my husband, nor I, could ever be one like it says in Genesis 2:24, **"the two shall become one flesh."** We are so different! He wants to go rock climbing on some high cliff. Or slide down the tallest waterslide he can find. Just leave me alone with my books.

"It took two to create you," said the Lord.

Wow! (I hope you have written down your answers in the questionnaire). I may need to reread Genesis 2:23-24.

> **Then Adam said, "This is now bone of my bones,**
> **And flesh of my flesh.**
> **She shall be called Woman,**
> **Because she was taken out of Man.**
> **Therefore a man shall leave his father and his**
> **mother, and shall cleave unto his wife: and they**
> **shall be one flesh**
> (Old King James without date).

I turned to my husband and asked, "what does cleave mean?"

He looked taken aback and said, "to cling" Then, said, "Look it up in the dictionary."

The smartphone dictionary said the verb cleave meant: "to split a molecule by breaking a particular chemical bond. Or a cell divided". It also means "to stick or to cling.". The Hebrew word "baqa" means "cleaving; breaking; tearing open."

I asked other Christian brothers and sisters what cleave meant, and they all said the same thing, "to Cling." You should have seen their faces when I ask, "then what does cleavage mean or cleaver?"

In the Old Testament, having more than one wife was not unusual for men. King David had eight named wives, according to the Bible, and his son, King Solomon, had 700 wives and 300 concubines (1 Kings 11:3). It seemed that once King Solomon cleaved to one wife, he found another wife to cleave to. The Bible states that King David's first 4 or 5 sons came from different wives.

I am spending some time on the meaning of cleaving, for we may not know what it means or what we have always thought it meant, but much more.

Let's go back to Adam. Adam might have thought about seed time a lot during his time alone. Look at the words he used when he saw the second Man; helpmate or help mete (a helper suited to, worth of, or corresponding to him), woman (the Man with the womb), cleave (cling to each other so close, you create another man or human being), and Eve, mother of all mankind (Genesis 2:18).

By combining all these meanings of Cleave in today's language, may mean something different than what we thought it meant when God told Adam to Cleve to his wife, and the two shall become one flesh? Could God have been telling Adam to have sex with his wife (Cleve), planting his seed in her so their seeds would split and become **their** one flesh (a child)? It might also explain why a man needs to decide between staying home with his parents or making his own home with a wife.

As I pondered all this, I realized why God put the 5th Commandment in with the other ten commandments. It always seemed out of place with the other commandments. **"Honor your father and mother, that your days may be long upon the land which the Lord your God gives you"** (Exodus 20:12 New King James).

God created Man in His image. Male and female. Man is to honor their Creator. Even though God created children perfectly in their mother's womb, they are born in their parent's images and are to honor and respect their parents. I don't know about you, but I would be afraid to talk disrespectfully against my God. And it should be the same way with children towards their parents. We should listen, obey, and respect their wishes or desires, just as we should with God. No wonder God put Exodus. 20:16 **"Honor your father and mother . . .".** And it is all because your father cleaved to your mother and became one . . . through you.

I was rebellious while growing up. I spoke out of frustration and hurt toward my parents. I wish I knew then what I had just learned about speaking against my parents. When I spoke against my parents, I spoke against myself since I was from their seeds. Their movements were in me. How I walked, got along with people, and my temperament; so many things that were instinctive in my parents were in me: my mother's easy-going nature and smile, my dad's love for children, and his deep thoughts. I look like my father but am built and stand like my mother.

When I was living at home, we adopted a stray cat that was pregnant. When the cat had her kittens, a car hit her. My sister nursed those little kittens with a doll bottle until they were on solid food. One of the kittens was a clone of her mother, with the same color and temperaments. She even held her tail straight up and was touchy when anyone touched it. She ruled those other little kittens and everything and everyone around her. All these things were not learned but passed down through her mother's seed, whom she had never set eyes on. It is the same thing with Man's seed, and we are to give our parents the same respect and honor as we give to God.

Have you heard a parent say to their child, "I wish you were like that neighbor kid down the block?" I am sorry, but your child is made up of your seed, not the seed down the block (at least, let's hope not). That parent would have been showing disrespect toward their child and themselves, who passed their seed to that child.

I have seen children scream at their parents, "I don't want to be like you!" However, when they have matured, they usually find themselves saying and doing things their parent did, and understanding their parents' logic, especially when they start planting their own seed. After all, they did come from the seeds of their parents. And they will pass these same traits to their children.

I have seen one parent act so disrespectfully towards the whole family that their seeds became rebellious and turned against the disrespectful parent to the point of turning away from the God of the Universe.

Many parents do not realize how their words and actions are

what shape their little seeds. They do not see them as an extension of themselves. Their seeds (or children) need to be nurtured, watered and protected until they are mature enough to leave, cleave and continue the next generation of seeds.

We no longer follow the covenant of unity anymore, for we do not understand what a covenant is with our parents or each other. We are ignorant of speaking against our spouses, children, and parents. In fact, in the Old Testament, if a man speaks against his wife in public, whom he cleaved to, he is speaking against her parents, too. She is their seed, their oneness. If what he says is false, he must pay her parents. If his words are accurate, the village men will stone her to death at her father's doorstep (Deuteronomy 22:13-21).

Leviticus 20:9 "For anyone who curses his father or mother shall surely be put to death. He has cursed his father or mother. His blood shall be upon him." (New King James Version)

CHAPTER 6

A COVENANT OF HONOR

PSALMS 78:1-8

(New Christian Version, 2006)

1. My people, listen to my teaching; listen to what I say.
2. I will speak using stories; I will tell secret things from long ago.
3. We have heard them and known them by what our ancestors have told us.
4. We will not keep them from our children; we will tell those who come later about the praises of the Lords. We will tell about his power and the miracles he has done.
5. The Lord made an agreement with Jacob and gave the teachings to Israel, which he commanded our ancestors to teach to their children.
6. Then their children will know them, even the children not yet born. And they will tell their children.
7. So they would all trust God and would not forget what he had done but would obey his commands.

8. **They would not be like their ancestors who were stubborn and disobedient.**

Proverbs 78:2-4 tells us to tell our children stories of God in our lives. Stories about what God has done in our family and friends' lives, in the hope our children will pass it on to their children with Biblical teachings.

I have two stories that I have told to my children, Sunday School Class, and anyone that will listen to them. I told them to my children so they would learn to live by God's laws and commands, hoping they would learn to trust God and obey them. To recognize His hand in their lives, too.

There are more than two, but they are the two I most enjoy telling. And I would like to tell them to you too.

The first great disappointment I can remember was when I was about five years old.

My family and I lived off the main highway with a long driveway. We called a long, dirt driveway a "lane."

One snowy night, a man came from the highway asking my dad if he could sleep on our porch to escape the snowy weather. My dad said, "No, but you can sleep in our car." My mom gave the man a blanket to keep him warm.

The next day the man was gone. There weren't even any footprints in the snow. The only thing that showed the man existed was that mama's blanket was folded neatly in the car with a small old fashion wedding band in the center of the folded blanket.

Even though I could still fit into a wash pan, my fingers were probably chubby, for that little gold wedding band fit perfectly on my ring finger. And I claimed it as mine.

A couple of days later, we visited my aunt, and I wanted to show her my new ring. She also lived down a lane. At the end of her lane, it turned to go around her house and to their dairy barn. Instead of going around the house, we parked in her front yard. I jumped out of the car with the excitement of a five-year-old, running as fast as possible to show off my ring. Before I knocked on her front door, I realized something was wrong. I looked down at my ring finger, and my precious ring was gone. It had fallen off in my excitement to show it to my aunt. I looked frantically across her large front yard where I had run. There was no way I could retrace my steps backward. I had to accept that my precious ring was lost.

The next time I felt that kind of loss was when I was 28. I had come back home to my roots after a broken relationship. I moved in with a childhood girlfriend. I fell in love with her little house. It felt like home. I moved in about the same time she obtained a new neighbor who was divorced with three children. With his three children and her one, it didn't take long for them to start wedding plans. They asked me if I wanted to buy her house, which I did, and I started doing what needed to be done to buy it.

Everything was going about as smoothly as possible when buying a HUD home. Every problem they tried to create was quickly eliminated. The last thing HUD housing does is check your credit report. In my entire 28 years, I have never thought about my credit report. Whenever I bought a car, someone was always helping me. But this house was something else. I felt God was helping me throughout this whole process of obtaining this house.

My credit report came in and showed that I had one bad credit report that would keep me from getting my beloved house. It showed I still owed the VA money for a college loan, which I had paid five or six years ago, but I needed proof! HUD told me where I needed to go to get it corrected. I immediately went to the VA office and explained my problem. They were as clueless as to what I should do as I was.

I went home crying on God's shoulder. "I thought this was what you wanted me to do," I cried. "I don't understand."

By the time I got to the little house, I had accepted my loss and God's will for me. When I got to the little house, I stopped on the street (a cul-de-sac) before pulling up in the driveway. I left the car to look at the beautiful little place I loved and called home. Standing on the street, looking at the little house, I finally decided to check the mailbox before pulling the car into the carport. I had gotten one piece of mail that day from the government showing that I had paid my VA loan off five years ago! I had my proof. Oh, what a God we serve.

I had lived in that little house for 10 years before I met and decided to remarry. Both of us were not rich, and between the two of us, we couldn't save up enough to buy rings. Much less one ring. We both felt the Lord would provide one for us, but our wedding date was getting closer and closer.

About two weeks before the wedding, my aunt called me. The first words out of her mouth were, "Bea, didn't you lose a ring here when you were little"?

"Yes, I did," I replied.

"Well, your uncle was poking around the back porch steps with his walking cane when he hit something hard. He bent down to see what it was it was a little gold wedding band. I remembered you had lost one once."

Oh, how I wanted that ring, but I wasn't going to lie to get it.

"Yes, I did, but I lost it in front of your house, not in the back," I reply.

"Lands sacks Bea" was her comeback, "we moved our house closer to the land over 20 years ago and added a back porch."

I sometimes wonder if that man came to our porch that snowy winter night over 30 years ago was one of God's angels to deliver that small wedding band to me and then buried it for a time when needed.

We all have stories we need to tell our children about how awesome God is to us. Do you tell your family stories to them? Or are we too busy to bother telling them to our children? Or too busy for them to be part of your life.

In the Old Testament, people knew how important telling their ancestry stories was to their children. Perhaps, when parents tell these stories to their children, they ask basic questions; like marriage, covenants, work ethics, honor, and where they came from, to name a few, which were passed down to their children and to their children's children. And to their children that had not yet been born. Things that people today do not think about or a majority do not know the reasoning for anymore, because both parents work in today's society. Therefore, what should be passed down to their children is lost.

I say this because simple questions were asked to adults, both Christians, and non-Christians; what is the reason for marriage, or why do people get married today? Depending on their age, I got different answers to these questions; to start a family; to become respectable since we are living together; not be alone; have someone to do things with; have someone to come home to; someone to care for or for someone to care for me; to be together. One person said their job required them to be married if there was any advancement in their career.

I especially enjoyed asking questions to people that seldom, if ever, went to church. They usually just looked at you with a completely blank looks on their face and at a loss for words. They understood you were supposed to get married, but not the why. They had no clue.

Christians should be known as the covenant people of God. But do Christians even know what a covenant is? And if they do know, did they teach it to their children? Have people thought about why being a homosexual is wrong? Not just because God hates it, but WHY God hates it? What about cleave? Did you understand its true meaning in marriage? I could go on and on about simple, basic things we take for granted and do not question. We go along with what the majority says it is, to the point that we forget the answer.

Today our youth is questioning these basic rules that have been passed down to them, and most Christian parents have no answers to why except, "because I told you so," or "because that is what the Bible says," or 'that is how it has always been so don't question it or rock the boat." The parents of today's youth have no answers to pass down, for they also are now groping in darkness. Psalms 78:5-8 says that our children will become increasingly rebellious and do things we never thought someone in our Christian families would ever do. They lack the knowledge of secret things that generations before them should have taught the younger generation. And if they do not know or understand the power and greatness of God, their Creator, how can they learn to honor their parents?

Chapter 4, "LOVE," stated that love was a covenant word, and therefore, marriage should be entered into as a covenant. If Christians understand this marriage covenant, I doubt the divorce rate would be as high as that of the unbeliever. Last I heard, it was a 60% divorce rate for both.

In the Old Testament, couples made a covenant when their fathers decided it was time for their children to start procreation, and the fathers were the ones that proclaimed the young couple as man and wife. Then the couple waits. This waiting period is what we might call being engaged today, ensuring they are making the right choice before walking down the aisle. But the young people in Biblical times did not have that choice as couples do today. Their marriage covenant meant more than being engaged. It meant being bound as a married couple with their words or agreement. If either one broke that covenant, the person that broke it would be put to death. That was how important a person's word was. This is also where we get "till death do we part." Mary, the mother of Jesus, is an excellent example of this. She was given to Joseph as a virtuous young woman for him to wife, and the next thing he knew, she was pregnant! He could have had her stoned to death on her father's doorstep because of their marriage covenant (American Standard, Deuteronomy 22:21-22, 2022). Tamar is another good example of "till death do we part." Her father-in-law wanted to burn her at the stake when he thought she was not a virtuous woman. Christians today do not seem to take their marriage vows seriously, nor their words.

When I was a child, people made their covenant with their words and a handshake, and there was no doubt their word would be kept. My dad was one of those people that you could take his word to the bank. He made a covenant with my mom to take care of her. If he made another covenant with another person, like borrowing money for a truck, he had it paid off at the covenant time. Today, we do not call it a covenant; we call it good character. People have a tough time honoring their commitment, whether verbally or on paper.

If we had been taught what a covenant was and how to keep it, the male's tool and the female's womb, "fe" to bring forth; the meaning of cleaving, how the two create one; and the fifth commandment, things might not be in such a mess in the world today and in our nation. Reread Psalms 78:1-8.

In the Old Testament, when their children's hormones started, parents already had that taken care of through marriage. This keeps unwanted and unplanned seeds of children coming into the world, especially when neither the young boy nor girl would think about breaking their covenant. They both knew what it meant if they did. The young son was taught the family business and usually worked with his father.

Therefore, thirteen and fourteen-year-olds were already in a marriage covenant. Their Biblical Wedding Ceremony happened when the two cleaved to one another to plant their seeds for the first time, and any other time they come together to plant their seeds. That was what the Biblical Marriage Ceremony is all about and still is in the eyes of God.

Love, usually, had nothing to do with whom you married. That came later. Age also did not have anything to do with marriage. Usually, it was young people, but not always. Tamar probably married men her age at the beginning, then was willing to marry a much younger man, but instead had her child with a much older man, her father-in-law. And look at Abraham. He was 137 years old when his first wife, Sarah, died. He remarried after her death and had seven more children (Genesis 25). His new wife had to be at least one hundred years younger than him. It must have been something other than love, like children or preserving man's seed.

We sing, "God never changes. He is the same yesterday, today, and tomorrow". Do we really believe that? I mean, Really, REALLY believe that? Or have we become more like the Baal worshipers?

The Biblical Wedding Ceremony is when two families come together and make a covenant with their children. A price is set for the young woman. The father of the young woman and the father of the young man were the ones that pronounced the couple man and wife (man and his Kallah). But the Biblical Wedding Ceremony happens when the two come together to plant their seeds for the first time.

This practice did not stop after the death of Christ. In fact, this practice was used to describe Christ's church as His Bride and He the Bridegroom. And yet, many of us do not understand it.

CHAPTER 7

THE BRIDE OF CHRIST

(Kallah)

Our church has a "candlelight service every year on the Sunday before Christmas, which my husband and I faithfully go to. It is calming and peaceful during a season that is so stressful.

One year the candlelight service was on Christmas Eve, and it felt exceptionally holy.

During this Candlelight Service, our pastor spoke on 1 Corinthians 11:17-31. "Being pure of heart." While listening to him, the Lord started opening my heart concerning the Marriage Ceremony.

A man would buy another man's daughter for a wife with money, livestock, or even precious jewels. Jacob worked for 14 years for his father-in-law's two daughters (Genesis 29: 16-30). The father, with a daughter, would become wealthy from the covenant the two families would make with each other. The daughter, or bride, would stay under her father's protection until the bridegroom had prepared a permanent place for their dwelling to raise their children. If a man paid a fortune for another man's daughter, there was no way he would not be coming back for his bride; they were married once the two families made the covenant for the daughter.

It was no different with Jesus. He asks our Father in Heaven for us . . . His church . . . His bride. Our father said yes. Then we had to say yes to Him. But God did not want what earthly fathers wanted, money, jewels, or livestock. His son would have to pay a more significant price for His bride, so she would know she was worthy of Him coming back for her. God, the father, wanted Jesus to pay for His bride with a blood sacrifice. His Body and Blood for His bride. His very life. God knew His Son's bride would not stay faithful, being bought with earthly possessions. Only through a blood sacrifice would she stay true. She would then know she was valued through her life on earth until He came to take her to His home in Heaven. He wanted us to partake of the "bread" that represented His body, the word of God, and the "wine" that represented the blood that He shed for His bride on the earth. His intimate, agape love Covenant. If He paid that price for His Bride, His Church, then we know He will come back for us after He finishes our mansion with many rooms. We are protected by the covering of his blood if we stay under God's laws or the body of Christ.

Christ is the perfect Bridegroom, a perfect Son, and He deserves no less from His bride; the church should also be perfect. Without spot or wrinkle. Whenever we, as a church, take our Lord's supper, we remember His payment for us and know He is coming back for us, His bride. But are we worthy of His love? Are we operating in His body? Do we have hate, anger, resentment, pride, the things the Lord hates, in our hearts? Are we worthy of being under His protection? Do we still have a love of a bride in our hearts for our Bridegroom? That is why the bridegroom paid such an enormous price for His bride. So, we do not forget.

The next time our church has communion or the Lord's Supper, I will sit in my pew holding this small piece of bread that represents Christ's body. Remember how His flesh on His back was torn to look like hamburger meat before nails were hammered into His hands and feet and wonder if I am worthy to be a bride of someone that took so much suffering and pain that he gave his very life. Oh, how He paid such a high price for me, His bride.

Then I will hold the cup of grape juice that represents His blood. The blood that dripped down on the ground from the nails pierced in His hands and feet, the spear that pierced His side . . . till He gave up His life for me. The bread—His word, the wine—His sacrificial blood . . .The price He paid for me . . .Your bride.

We are now in the most critical part of our young marriage to Christ the Son. The young bride is still under the protection of her father while getting to know the bridegroom. She is preparing, learning, and getting things ready for a new life with her Bridegroom when He returns to retrieve His young bride when He finishes that mansion for us. Oh, how I want to be worthy of Him, a bride without spots or wrinkles.

I did say a young bride, didn't I? Yes, I did. Because a bride that is 50, 60, or even one hundred years old is young to the Lord compared to eternity.

CHAPTER 8

THE FAMILY TREE

I was reading Adam's lineage when I came across a man named Jubal, the father of all who played stringed instruments and pipes (Genesis 4:21). I often wondered if this is where we get the word Jubilee. I then turned to the front of the Bible, where there was an empty family tree. I remembered my grandmother writing down birthdates, weddings, and deaths of family members, which was passed down to my uncles' family to continue filling it out. It was their way of keeping track of the family lineage before the internet. Today, families donate their bibles with their family trees to historical societies.

As I sat looking at the tree, wondering how long the printed family tree would continue being in the Bibles. So many people are marrying and remarrying, with very few children who are whole siblings and some who do not even know their fathers. As I continued looking at the blank family tree, I realized families were growing smaller and smaller, which meant the world's population was growing smaller and smaller, too. My mother has three children. Only one of those three has produced great-grandchildren. And there are only two of them.

How did everything change so much from what God intended? When did the Biblical marriage ceremony change to what it is today? And when did man decide that populating the earth was not important anymore?

Since the Bible stops at Acts and the Letters of the Apostles, I had to go to the internet. The most helpful place for me was "the early church and marriage." What you may find a year ago, you may not be able to find today. But the information you see today will only add to what you did find from previous searches. So let me give you the basics of what I found from my research.

After the crucifixion of Christ (Matthew 27) and the martyr of Steven (Acts 7), the believers fled all over Judah and Samaria. They fled to Damascus, Antioch, the Catacombs, and caves; hard to get to places in the mountains, and many even fled to pagan towns to hide from the persecutors that were sure to find them. The believers wanted to be ready for persecution, which was sure to come unless Christ came for them first. Therefore, many new believers studied the teachings of Christ and the Apostle's letters fervently. These men became indignant whenever some devout believers saw a young couple in their group pledge to each other. They felt these young people should be studying, preparing for their persecutors or Christ's return, not starting families! The world was populated enough. These devout believers had forgotten God's first command to mankind. To populate the earth.

The criticism got so bad for these young married people that they went to the leader in their community. The leader was usually the man the people gravitated to when they fled their persecutors, and he was considered the father of that community. Later the fathers in the different communities were called Saint, meaning someone with high standards. The father would say something to these devout men, and things calmed down for these young people for a while, and then condemnation would rise back up, making them feel like second-class citizens again.

Sometime in 900 A.D., the first marriage ceremony, as we know it, was performed. This ceremony had not been used since 2300 B.C. in Mesopotamia, about the time of the "Tower of Babel."

When the Believers reached Rome, they were called Christians and saw an opportunity to convert many pagans to Christ. They formed a place to worship and realized all the other little Christian communities and towns, should be under one umbrella for protection. They needed some way to do this and control these people, and the best way to do that was to have people be married by a Father; the Greek word for Father in Rome was Pope.

These Fathers in Rome refused to marry anyone that was a close family member, like first or second cousins, or anyone that had to do with Godparents. This caused a closeness in the family unit in these different communities to start breaking down, for most of these small communities were made up of close family members. First, second and third cousins, aunts and uncles, nephews, and nieces were not uncommon to marry one another. Therefore, the church made an extra effort to make sure couples wanting to be married were not marrying anyone in their own families. The phrase "if there is anyone who has any reason why this young couple should not be married, speak now or forever hold your peace" comes from this.

Later the church refused to marry anyone in the same community because most were family members. This caused the family closeness to become even more fractured.

Some people just said they were married without going to the Pope. The church leaders eventually passed a law saying a person must have two witnesses to be able to marry. Later the church turned over the marriage license to the government, and the government, also, saw this as an opportunity to control the people.

It was in the early 1900s that the United States passed a law stating that married couples had to have a marriage license before the government even recognized them as married. In 1954, India passed a similar law.

The closeness of the family unit seems to have disappeared entirely, by then. And so has the importance of the seed of man.

People don't know who God or his Son, Christ, is anymore. And the seed of man is gobbled up by our enemy, Satan, through drugs, abortion, sex trafficking, rapes, homosexuals, and so many other things.

Because of the loss of the family unit, I have seen many couples adopt other men's seeds. Giving those little seeds love, security, and protection, a chance in life that they wouldn't have had with their natural parents. And you would never know that they weren't their seeds, for those little seeds completed the family unit.

I have a son married to a woman with six children. Only one of those six is from his seed. He is now taking care of two of his stepdaughter's sons. His wife is taking college classes, and if not in classes, she is studying. Therefore, those little boys are left with him most of the time, and he is the only one they can depend on for security. In every way, they are his grandchildren, and he is their grandpa. They complete him as a family unit. They are bonded together through their love and trust.

It is the same in the Old Testament. When a man marries a woman, the woman is automatically adopted as a daughter of his family. She caused her husband and his family to be complete by bringing children into the family. She was adopted as their child, even though she was not of their seed. She is known as their son's "Kallah."

When we accept Christ as our Savior, our bridegroom, we are adopted by God as his child. We make Him complete and become part of a more prominent family that gives us love and security from a harsh world.

The sun is still going around the earth, the moon, and stars, are still in the sky, and the grass is still growing and producing seeds. Animals are still procreating, both on land and in the sea. But man is not, as God told him to do. Nor are they continuing to cleave to each other--or perhaps they are, just not as God intended for them.

If something happened to my husband and I was left alone, I am not sure I could enter another man's home or have a man enter my home to live as husband and wife without a marriage license because of my indoctrination. It may not be wrong, but as my mother would say, we are to follow the laws of the land if it isn't against God's law.

So how do people become married? I think that is something you must decide for yourself. Whatever you decide, remember that marriage is a covenant between you and God. And don't make a judgment if someone you know does not have a license.

I am glad my daughter was married by a Pastor. But instead of asking them if they would take each other as husband and wife, it would have been nice if he asked them instead, **"are the two of you ready to enter this world together, as man and wife, by being an example of Christ's love in a world that doesn't know what His love is"**?

We are Christ's Bride. We have walked down the aisle and made a covenant with Him; by giving our life to Him. We became God's children, and the love we have for Him, and He for us should be pouring out to our spouse and the fallen world around us. Now we wait for God the Father to tell His Son, Jesus, when the time is right for Him to bring His Bride to their new home.

WORKS CITED

American Standard Bible. (2022). Retrieved from Bible.com: https://www.bible.com/bible/12/GEN.1.ASV

Christian Standard Version. (2022). Retrieved from Bible.com: https://www.bible.com/bible/1713/GEN.1.CSB

New Century Version. (2022). Retrieved from Bible.com: https://www.bible.com/bible/105/GEN.1.NCV

New International Version. (2022). Retrieved from Bible.com: https://www.bible.com/bible/111/GEN.1.NIV

Newman, H. (1965, February 17). *The Birds and the Bees By Brenda Lee.* Retrieved from Second Hand Songs: https://secondhandsongs.com/performance/120694

The Holy Bible Concordance. (No Year). Cleavland: The World Publishing Company.

The Holy Bible, English Standard Version. (2001). Crossway, Good News Publishers.

The Holy Bible, English Standard Version. (2008). Wheaton, IL: Crossway Books.

The Holy Bible, King James Version. (n.d.).

The Torah. (1962). Philidelphia: Jewish Publication Society of America.

World Messianic Bible, Leviticus 18. (2022, 12 15). Retrieved from Bible.com: https://www.bible.com/bible/1209/LEV.18.WMB